© 2022 Stephanie Henson

In The Right Lane

ISBN: 9798363449710

Stephanie Henson

IN THE RIGHT LANE

FInding Your Path Through Poetry
Helping kids navigate life on the road to happiness.

In The Right Lane

Finding Your Path Through Poetry

Stephanie Henson

KATHRYN AND MATTHEW - STAY IN THE RIGHT LANE. WORK HARD. DON'T LET ANYONE DERAIL YOUR DREAMS.

THANK YOU TO MY FAMILY WHO MADE THIS POSSIBLE.

Contents

Before we begin, a poem for the parents...

The Captain

You have a job,
steer children on a path,
over hills and through muddy waters,
carefully, with focused intent.
A beautiful future awaits them if:
good decisions are made,
picking a lane,
staying on course,
following the route,
navigating inevitable detours.
Do not let anyone derail their plans:
You are their Captain.

A New School Year

Twilight skies emerge from Summer chaos.
The subtle glow calls out to the chilled air of Fall.
Cicadas silenced, bats flutter in the distance —
A calm settles across the landscape,
as children are tucked snug into their beds,
holding onto the last bit of warmth,
clutching blankets and dreams.
Waiting for the start of the school year.

Holding Onto Summer

Holding onto firefly-lit nights,
crickets chirping and hopping in flight.
Holding onto twinkling starry skies,
the sight of wishes flying high.
Holding onto marshmallows, melting on a stick,
a frightfully gooey treat that does the trick.
Holding onto sleeping bags: tucked in warm and tight,
dream inside backyard tents under bright moonlight.
Holding memories of summer days,
where chilly air takes over from heat haze.

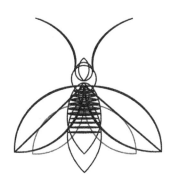

Night Before School

I toss and turn, try to embrace this time,
new year at school, it could be my prime:

An opportunity to pursue my dreams,
not sit in the background wishing, it seems.

I need to find my voice, stay in my lane,
work on the things I most wish to attain.

Carve out a path to make myself whole,
to find direction and take back control.

Whatever disappointments in the past,
I was not always destined to be last.

This is the year I break out of my shell,
let other students see what I do well.

So please, God, let me sleep and be ok,
let tomorrow be great drama-free day:

A fresh start, where I find a cool new tribe,
a whole new me with a confident vibe!

Who am I kidding? I am freaking out!
I am a wreck and I will fail, no doubt.

Why do I do this to myself? Allow the spiral.
Mustn't do something stupid and go viral.

Just calm down, I tell myself, you can do this.
It's just school, and not meant to be pure bliss.

Your besties are all in the same boat too:
You can do anything: a winning crew.

I look into the mirror and I say,
I am unstoppable and will do great today.

Nothing to lose and everything to gain.
Dreams can come true if you just use your brain.

In The Same Boat

We are all in the same boat,
paddling from class to class,
trying not to fall overboard
as the halls fill up with worry,
no navigation system at hand,
lost in a sea of unfamiliar faces,
hopelessly looking for an anchor to steady the surge.
Rogue waves of emotion consume—
nervous
excited
scared
It all blends and swirls in a pool of panic.
The tides of anxiety rise,
swept away by the overwhelming situations of the day:
What's worse in school?
The need for arm floaties, or drowning in doubt?
Tough call!
But you are your own lifeguard,
protect yourself and your feelings,
dip toes into the unknown carefully,
and swim in the direction of your dreams.
We are charting the same course to confidence.
We are all in the same boat.

New

New school
New clothes
New shoes
New backpack
New teachers
New classes
New books
New supplies
New locker
New rules
New friends
A new adventure awaits!

Worries

Worries, worries go away,
don't come back another day.
I am young and have things to do,
I can't be constantly thinking of you.
So please find somewhere else to go,
for I am confident, this much I know.
Your doubts that creep into my head,
will not keep me up late in bed.
I will not let waves make my tummy rough,
I know just who I am, and that's enough.
So no more worries for this smart girl,
off to explore this big wide world.

The Bus

The dreaded school bus,
smells like sweat and feet,
makes me want to fuss,
regretting that Mom made me eat.

Each bump and turn brings us closer to it,
my stomach lurches and my face feels hot,
friends next to me giggle and sit,
I wonder what great advice they got.

My mom told me to show people what I can do,
not to be shy and afraid to loom large.
but I'm not even sure who I am or what to pursue,
this will be a year for me to take charge.

The bus comes to a stop and I can hear some girls sneer,
they looked at someone's bag and seemed to whisper,
I'm guessing their backpacks are designer,
anger levels rise and I will protect my soul sister.

Here we go again, cant get away from those who bully,
mean girls who thrive on making others feel bad,
they surely can not love themselves fully,
girls who hate on other girls are just sad.

The Flute Playing Mathematical Artist Who Runs!

When I grow up, I want to be,
something that I can't yet see.

Blaze a trail across a path,
maybe do something involving math.

But I kind of like music too,
perhaps a mathematician who plays the flute.

Then again, art is neat,
a flute playing mathematician who draws would be a treat.

Yet, gym class is the most fun,
how about a mathematician, flute loving, artist who can
run?

I guess the possibilities are quite endless,
being whatever I want to be is tremendous.

Heroes

Heroes don't always wear capes.
Most times they wear everyday clothing:
Like a police uniform to protect and serve.
Or fireman's gear, complete with an oxygen tank.
Doctors can flex a white coat as they take your temperature.
Teachers can wear dresses or a suit by the chalkboard.
Perhaps a tall Chef's hat while serving soup to the homeless.
Construction workers build futures while wearing bright neon vests.
How about regular clothes worn by mom as she takes care of you during the day.
Or business casual attire as Dad provides for his family.
What kind of hero do you want to be?

School Construction Zone

Don't turn your back on who you want to become,
be ready to show up every day and work hard.
The road is long & paved with detours,
finding your path along the way is part of the job.
Keep U-Turns to a minimum,
school can be rough and a tough place to crack,
don't let rumors break you down.
You may need a tarp to protect the heart,
but remember, dirt can't smear if you clean up messes.
You control the leaks that burst,
no one can flood your eyes with tears.
The learning site is yours in the pursuit of happiness,
your dreams are valid and important.
Go hammer them out no matter what,
no one can stand in your way.
Dig deep.
You are a bulldozer of purpose!

Kites

Kites dance in the sky,
swirling back and forth with silliness,
and soaring high with strength.
Evidence of perseverance and a push of power,
once lifeless, now a spectacle to behold.
Don't let anyone hold you down,
with the wind to your back,
find your force —
Take off and fly.

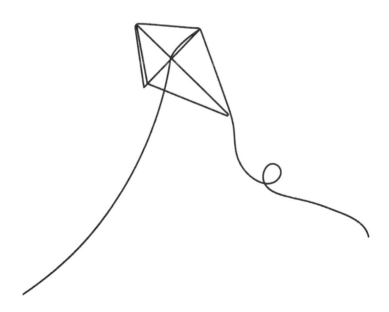

Land of Good Fortune

Fairy wings flutter with pixie dust,
a magical sprinkle of prayers answered,
where the wishes of children are carried away,
on the backs of mythical creatures,
to a land where wonder and good fortune prevails.
Believe in miracles and a higher power,
and enchanting tales can come true.

Bent

Someday I'll find my people who will appreciate the real
me.
The me who marches to the beat of pots and pans.
The me who cheers with pom poms strung from ribbons.
The me who builds planes out of cardboard boxes.
The me who makes phones out of cans and strings.
The me who crafts swords out of sticks.
The me who creates forts out of couch cushions.
The me who is a little bent in an unbent world.

A Big COLORFUL Life

I'm small but my feelings are big,
I live a colorful life.
Sometimes I can't explain how I feel,
so the colors help it all make sense to me.

Like today; I'm having a RED day.
I'm angry and mad but not sure why.
I see red and all I want to do is scream into my pillow.
Dad says to breathe through it and I'll be alright.

Maybe tomorrow will be a YELLOW day.
Those are the best.
Bright clear skies give way to happy smiles,
where you can play all day under the warmth of the yellow
sun.

GREEN days are reminders of the things you want but can't
have.
The green-eyed monster sometimes takes hold and won't
let go!
Mom says jealousy is a wasted emotion.
She's probably right.

Then there can be GRAY days.
Days where things aren't necessarily black or white,
but somewhere in between.
Where confused gray clouds hang low, rumbling in the sky.

There's always a chance of a BLUE day.
Where sadness creeps in unexpectedly,
while the rainy day blues can be a pain,
there's always a chance of rainbows after the rain.

And RAINBOW days are my absolute favorite.
Where all of the colors come together,
for a sensory show in the sky.
Where you can be proud of whoever you are,
and however you feel!

Live a Big COLORFUL Life!

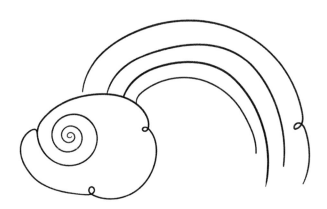

Empathy Recipe

A dash of empathy.
A pinch of comfort.
A sprinkle of kindness.
A scoop of understanding.
Mixed with compassion,
is a glitter bomb of happiness to the bullied ones.
A rising confection of acceptance,
for kids who are imploding from rejection.
It's a magical recipe passed down to those who need it the
most.

Production

Life is one big production.
Direct your present.
Write your future.
Sing your dreams.
Produce fine art.
Dance with innocence.
Photograph with purpose.
Act with dignity.
Edit when needed,
For freedom of expression and
a chorus of encouragement,
leads the orchestra of change.
on the biggest stage.
Leave drama at the door,
character is everything.

The Music in My Head

Sometimes the music in my head isn't really music at all.

Sometimes it's your voice repeating on a loop that I can do it.

Sometimes it's the echo of your celebration yell when I achieve my goals.

Sometimes it's the vibration of clapping in the bleachers when I make the last shot.

Sometimes it's the whistle of encouragement right before a big performance.

Sometimes it's the melody of us laughing in the car on the way home.

Sometimes it's the hum of the way you hug me at the end of a long day.

The music in my head is having you as my biggest cheerleader in life!

Face Painting

Brushstrokes over my face
Paint a picture of who I want to be
Creative streaks of artwork
Stroking upwards on bare cheekbones
Natural features enhanced
Become exaggerated with each pass
A flare for the dramatic
Will I be . . .
An insect?
An animal?
A superhero?
Hear a voice coming
Uh oh
Maybe she won't notice
But
Can't hide behind mommy's makeup

Reflection

Stare at the mirror on the wall,
don't recognize this kid at all.

So many changes coming at me fast,
pride and confidence are things of the past.

I need to replace bad thoughts with good,
as hard as it is, I know I should.

It's tough enough just being me,
being kinder to myself will set me free.

On a journey to embrace my many quirks,
can't worry about any jerks.

Those who know me will understand,
this is a phase where we all will land.

So I'm getting comfortable in my skin,
accepting differences from within.

I am beautiful and you are too,
not much else to say or do!

Turtle Crossing

A turtle crossing sign along the bend,
bright yellow and reflective.
Images of mama and baby displayed,
their shells can only shield so much.
It says maneuver with care.
We encounter it daily in our route,
but never once have any of us seen a turtle,
not yet hauling out of the pond to nest.
Still, we continue to use caution.
To protect other species is a responsibility.
All people need to adopt such heart,
to make the world a safer place.

Baby Birds

An egg in the nest,
hatched into a tiny baby bird.
Protected and shielded until it's ready to fly.
Fledgling birds learn to work it out on their own,
often taking lots of practice to act on this instinct.
With encouragement from their parents,
they take off and soar.
So if you stumble at first –
Be aware of the baby birdies
and know that you can fly high too!

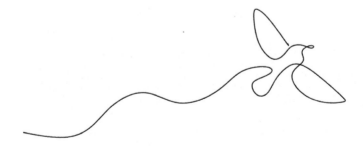

Lightning Bugs

Lightning bugs mesmerize in the darkness,
flicker and glow intermittently.
Waiting for a chance to shine.
A magical display of power.
Biding their time to make an entrance,
and enchant little ones within dusk's lush terrain.
Sometimes you need to seize the opportunity,
and make your move at the perfect moment in time.
Remember . . .
Lightning bugs in the daytime are just bugs.

Like A Tree

I want to be like a tree.
To stand tall and spread my limbs.
To shield others from the harsh elements of the world.
To have a strong trunk that identifies my unique parts.
To have roots that keep me grounded and nourished.
To shed my insecurities like leaves in the winter.
To withstand the storms that come.
To move to the beat of nature's drum.
To display colorful expressions of growth.
To bloom new every year.
I want to be like a tree.

Shooting Stars

In the darkness of night,
staying awake is a fight.

Watch shooting stars streak through the sky,
wondering where it is they fly?

Where do the stars land and what can they do,
to make a little kid's wishes come true?

Seems so unlikely but I wish anyway,
and I will continue to do so everyday.

Until my wish finds a home and comes back to me,
for then I will celebrate with beaming glee.

Wishes

A penny in a fountain.
11:11 on the clock.
A dandelion in the grass.
Candles on a birthday cake.
A ladybug on your sleeve.
Starlight star bright, first star you see tonight.
Make your wishes often.
May they come true in spectacular fashion.

Chasing Bubbles

Bubbles take flight in the wind,
shiny iridescent spheres of delight.
Sometimes can see a glimmer of a rainbow on the surface,
as they float up up up and away,
Kids chase the excitement with glee,
trying to capture that elusive feeling of freedom.
Only to find when it's nearly caught,
it's gone.
But . . .
Keep running,
Keep trying,
Keep reaching!
Fly high, towards the sky.
Chase those bubbles.
Chase big dreams!

Why Wouldn't I?

I will hang your dreams from the moon for the world to
see.
Why wouldn't I?

I will pin your desires to the sun to burn alongside me.
Why wouldn't I?

I will attach your wishes to a shooting star so it comes to
be.
Why wouldn't I?

I will shadow you like the clouds to protect thee.
Why wouldn't I?

You are everything I need.

The Space In Between

I am small,
but have big feelings.

I am young,
but want to be older.

I am smart,
but unsure of myself.

I am sunshine,
but can rain tears of frustration.

I am ready to fly upward,
but stuck in the space between.

In My Feelings

Um . . .

I feel funny
In my tummy

I feel dread
In my head

I feel upset
In my chest

But . . .

I can breathe
And gain peace

I can try
And not cry

I can rebound
And calm down

Then . . .

I will be
A happy me

Bubble Over

So many emotions!
A volcano simmering on the surface.
My feelings start to bubble over –
Blub
Plop
Glurb
But I am sure not to let them pop!
Inhale
Whoosh
Breathe
Keep control of the situation.
To avoid any eruptions!

Nature's Soundtrack

It was a rainy day when I heard,
nature's soundtrack on a loop.
Droplets of water dancing on the roof,
howling of the wind's gleeful approval.
Tapping of leaves as precipitations weighs.
Birds chirping in tempo from the safety of their nest.
Geese cackling at the ripples of the pond.
The buzz of bees playing trumpets against windows.
Screaming clicks of the cicadas burrowing down.
Thunder drums beats of rhythmic patterns in the sky.
Lightning provides epic strobes of pyrotechnics,
of this melodic performance of Mother Earth -
I want to perform in nature's concert too.

Sunflowers Stand Tall

A sunflower stands tall in the field.
Strong green stalk with thick leaves reaching outward,
almost in a power pose.
Bright yellow petals extend from a brown floret center,
brings a smile to all.
The sunflowers withstand the elements.
Harsh rain can bend and halt their growth.
Yet, the flowers still manage to bloom,
even with nature's tears raining down.
Somehow they always face the sun and shine.
Be like a sunflower.

Ballerina Cherry Tree

A grande Weeping Cherry Tree sways,
tall in stature, a presence in and of itself,
long lines extend into the world around it.
Arched branches mimic ballerina feet,
elegantly stretch down to the ground.
Vivid leaves dance effortlessly with flow.
The feel of tutu petals spinning in the wind,
often backstage to more vibrant stars,
Green at first, on point to bloom.
Thus, once a year - a chance to shine.
Company of pure pink petals flourish,
pirouette & jete around the surface.
To the beat of seasons changing,
nature's choreography dazzles.
A position to transform,
velvet beauty of rebirth.

The Lovely Garden

There is a garden at the park,
that gets a little testy after dark.

Every flower wants to be the best,
each day they are put through the test.

Sunny the Sunflower and Rosie the Rose,
are always front & center to strike a pose.

Tula the Tulip and Dee the Daisy,
flaunt their gorgeous petals like crazy.

Cassie the Cactus feels left out,
she is different from the others no doubt.

At night is when she begins her taunts,
love and admiration is all she wants.

She allows their beauty upset her,
so she teases them to feel better.

With each jab, the other flowers wilt,
in an instant, Cassie feels guilt.

She just wants to be part of the group,
to be a special part of the flower troop.

Cassie decides she doesn't like how she feels,
so, lifting up others will help her heal.

Cassie says sorry and helps them stand tall,
kind words are helpful after all.

Everyone is special, even a cactus with thorns,
we all possess great gifts when we are born.

Cassie learned that she's unique and true,
and that the garden needs her too.

Garden of Change

Forces at play,
working behind the scenes.
To plant perennial seeds,
here or there, anywhere.
Let the universe guide,
to a destination meant to be.
What's needed in the moment?
A work of serendipitous nature,
find land exactly where you should plant roots,
and nurture the soul.
To grow a beautiful garden of change.

Tree of Life

A beautiful tree that once stood tall,
the leaves change colors and gradually fall.

An empty vessel where beauty once lived,
still has so many gifts to give.

Solid bark is the protective shell,
that hides the fragile insides so well.

An awkward transition on the outside,
is necessary for growth on the inside.

The seasons change and transformation looms,
new buds and petals begin to bloom.

An important shift that has come full circle,
A central theme that's so universal.

Whether you are a tree or a teen,
will always have stages of in between.

But as long as you are strong and true,
there is nothing that you can't see through.

Mud

Trudging through the mud of the day,
Stuck in mounds of boredom.
Footprints within the earth,
not yet inspired.
Staining the soles of sneakers,
sinking into sticky ground,
Need a way to move forward,
so take off those shoes,
And run towards a better tomorrow.

Gossip Season

Words fly through the air like pollen.
Choking on particles of truth.
An allergic reaction that somehow spreads.
Must fight to breathe.
The right to inhale belief.
Wipe your tear-stung eyes.
Trust in crystal clear skies.
For you are your own cure,
to endure —
Gossip season.

Heavenly Justice

Bullies rarely play by the rules,
yet their victims are put on trial.
Abuse of power to judge others.
Found guilty of just existing in their world.
Trapped in a jail of jitters.
Sentenced to daily doses of mean words,
rely on imagination to escape.
Maybe they'll arrest someone else and release me.
Maybe they'll break these chains and I can be free.
Maybe I'll live a normal life and put this behind and be.
A second chance to embrace who I am.
They should be held accountable for their crimes on the
innocent,
but the world isn't always fair.
Walk away and never look back,
for I'm stronger because of what I went through.
Let justice prevail from above.

Power (Acrostic)

Prepare
Own It
Work Hard
Every Day
Repeat

Finding Your Voice

On a journey to find what was lost,
it lives deep inside but rarely comes out.
Holding back somehow–
Caught
Silenced
Quiet
Trains of thought chug along, but get stuck on the tracks.
Ideas run wild, but get tripped up at the finish line.
It's in there, charging to the surface, waiting to boom with
surprise-
A strong voice
A silly voice
A caring voice
A friendly voice
A loving voice
A loud voice
To be you without fear.
Look within for your voice,
to the parts of you hidden away,
Found
Rescued
Saved
Be proud of who you are,
your words are important.
Let it out for the world to hear!

Beach Tales

The ocean is in constant conversation.
Roaring with enthusiasm over its ideas.
Talks with mermaids and sea urchins.
The seagulls dip into the action.
We are not privy to their private tales.
A rhythm to the banter,
an ebb and flow,
in and out,
Until the ocean speaks only to itself.
Be careful how much is spilled,
Or you could be swimming alone.

Anchor of Hope

A ship floating aimlessly,
lost at sea.
Fish flopping out of water on deck,
went off course in a storm,
Drifting further and further away.
Dolphins dive in the distance.
No life jacket or lifeboats onboard.
Rogue waves of worry crash on the outside,
deep fear resides on the inside.
Must radio for help –
Can not steer back to shore alone.
Maps are blurred from the rain.
Drop the anchor with hope,
that rescue workers will lead the vessel back home.
Always look for the helpers.

Tween Geometry

Square peg,
round hole.

A diamond in the rough,
but a star in the making.

Outside of the social circle,
yet inside the drama triangle.

If feelings are stuck in a box,
then one can never break out.

All I want is a straight path onward,
to be my own person.

An arrow shooting forward,
intersecting with my dreams.

A confusing set of terms to prove I'm ready —

To point in the right direction,
of this parallel tween universe.

Twisting Dreams

What happens when a dream dies?
Is there a funeral or speech to give?
A dream can change without warning.
Twists & Turns
Dissed & Burned
Alter the original plan.

But . . . Can . . . Also . . .

Morph into a brand new goal.
Maintain progress
Sustain success
Transform the future into something greater than expect-
ed.
The world works in mysterious ways.
Trust the process.

Human

Missed the game winning shot.
Let the last goal go by you.
Struck out with the bases loaded.
Forgot the words to your chorus solo.
Fell out of a turn in your dance.
Misspelled a word in the Spelling Bee.
Got a bad grade on a test.

Don't fret,

You're human after all.

And humans aren't perfect.

But if you work hard and practice,
it may be better the next time around.
Don't give up!

That's A Win

Never feel good enough,
always the one left out.
Things are so tough,
want to scream and shout.

Many fun things about me,
to share with the group.
If they had a chance to see,
maybe I'd be in the loop.

Until then I will stand tall,
learning and growing from within.
I'm a good person after all,
at the end of the day, that's a win.

Field Day

Today is Field Day at school,
I'm on the blue team and I will rule.
The awards will be mine to take,
winning will be a piece of cake!

First event is bean bag toss,
in the buckets, throw like a boss.
There is nothing I can not do!
I am so much better than you.

No one could catch me in the race,
I screamed "I'm the best" in their face.
This day is going just fine,
oh that trophy will be mine.

Basketball is next and I'm a star,
I hogged the ball, near and far.
Go up for my shot and OH NO!
I landed hard with a groan.

I heard the rip before I hit,
my pants were definitely split!
Giggles and screams heard everywhere,
as I stood in my underwear.

Who's having a field day now?
The kids pointed and said, "HOLY COW!"
My face flushed red at the gaffe.
Then suddenly, I stood up and laughed!

I guess sometimes you need to come down to earth,
A serving of humble pie never hurts.
From now on I'll be nice and fair,
be a better teammate and a friend who cares.

Sports Dreams

Goals at the soccer stadium
Three-pointers on the basketball court
Setting records in the pool
Penalty shots at the hockey rink
Home Runs on the baseball diamond
Touchdowns on the football field
Aces at the tennis pavilion
Holes in one on the golf course
Jumping hurdles on the track
Pirouettes in the studio
A perfect 10 in the gym

It takes hard work,
It takes discipline,
It takes time,

You are the focus!
You can do it!
You got this!

Don't let anyone derail your dreams!

Champion

The silky ribbon is placed around my neck,
the cool feel of the medal graces my chest,
to stand tall on the podium,
A pillar of hard work and strength.
Nothing comes easy,
hours of practices,
sacrifices to my social life,
just a kid but —
with this gleaming token of accomplishment,
pride and happiness overwhelm,
for I have earned the honor,
of being a champion.
And I am not ready to let go of this feeling just yet!

Sports Shoes

Soccer cleats are way too muddy to keep neat on my feet.

Ballet slippers bend and fray as I dance everyday.

Baseball spikes kick up dirt and more, rounding bases to score.

Hockey Skates glide on a single blade, creating a path to goals I've made.

Basketball sneakers squeak and cause a ruckus, as I fast break to the bucket.

Gymnastics only calls for bare feet; to tumble, flip, jump, and leap.

Track shoes are really fun, hugging the turf so you can swiftly run.

So many options out there to see, gotta pick the one that is right for me.

Lollipops

Luscious lollipops line the lane,
A path of sublime sugar cane.

Curves and leads to a candy fort,
Filled with chocolate bars and a torte.

I can eat my way through this place,
And wipe the evidence from my face.

A magical hideout just for me,
A vision of what dreams can be.

I imagine myself in a land,
Where candy never leaves my hand.

Sometimes life can be sweet,
Filled with imagination, love, and yummy treats.

Breakfast Rush

Getting ready for school is no big deal,
Mom makes sure that I eat my meal.
Toast, fruit, and yogurt too,
Mom says there's so much to do.

I am busy clearing my plate,
Mom packs my bag so I won't be late.
Next I need to find something to wear,
Mom has clothes laid out on a chair.

Today is my trumpet lesson- almost forgot,
Mom has it packed in a special spot.
Books, folders, and pencils in a bunch,
Mom has also packed my lunch.

I don't get why it's so tough,
Mom says we need to rush.
Get in the car, but I forgot my mask.
Mom runs back inside in a flash.

Now we have all that we need,
Mom looks like she needs to breathe.
Get to school and I say goodbye,
Here Mom looks a wee bit fried.

We got to school with time to spare,
Mom says it helps to be prepared.
I'm all set to rock this day,
Mom sips her coffee as she pulls away.

Backpack

I'm heavy.
Often slung over a shoulder.
Able to view the school day from a different lens.
I am the keeper of all things needed to learn:
Packets
Pencils
Paper
Can even fit a computer in my sleeve!
Loaded and lugged around.
I see when you are stressed.
I feel when you are worried.
I hear when laughter finally breaks through.
The whole time, I give peace of mind,
that I have everything you need.

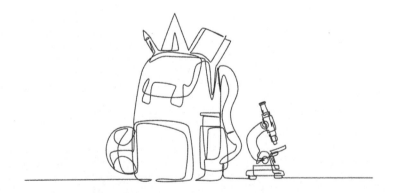

Undelivered - A Message From Your Phone

Little fingers dancing across my surface,
rhythmically tapping to the beats of games, apps, & texts.
I light up at the information provided,
and the ease of which it's absorbed.

But with my presence and interest, there's guilt,
kids should be outside enjoying nature and indulging the
senses.
Watching plastic bags twirl & flap in the wind with bliss,
reading stories that transport the imagination to places
beyond the box.

All of these immersive experiences,
yet they are glued to my screen,
endless yearning and wanting for more.
They are completely obsessed with me,
I don't know if I should feel pride or regret.

FOMO

Fear of Missing Out
On the phone
Scrolling through time
Living through others
Forced perceptions
Skewed perspective
Locked in on a screen
Missing the open air
Real connections absent
Disconnected from reality
Tunnel vision
Then . . .
Ironically . . .
You end up REALLY missing out!

Night Reading

Under my covers with a flashlight,
reading the rest of my book tonight.

Mom says it's time to be done,
but want to see how this ends and who won.

Tales help me escape into the night,
during times where resting is a fight.

I can lay in my bed and imagine a land,
far far away on a beach with white sand.

OR

A cabin in the woods with a spooky ghost,
nervous energy is what I love the most.

OR

Fairies in the garden, doing powerful things,
sweet smelling magic dust coating their wings.

OR

Maybe in a castle with Kings and Queens,
the pages of books, it's all in between.

Stories are a special gift to keep.
As I drift off to a peaceful sleep.

Shadows

By the soft glow of the nightlight,
my bedroom comes alive.

A natural exhibit of light and dark,
objects break through in motion.

The rays cast a spell on the walls,
a blank canvas into a mural of shadow art.

Not afraid of what's displayed,
no ghosts or goblins to be found.

Eyes playing tricks on me,
make me double take as I lie awake in my bed.

Where ceiling fan blades turn into helicopter propellers,
taking flight across the sky.

Beams bounce off the closet into an outline of a rocket,
launched into outer space.

The angles of the TV mimic a race car in my sights,
zooming and vrooming through the room.

In the corner, a kite flies errantly through the clouds,
climbing and soaring with the force of the wind.

My own shadow does not scare,
imagination comforts and adventures await.

Until I close my eyes,
and dream a little dream.

Time

Seconds turn into minutes,
Minutes turn into hours,
Hours turn into days,
Days turn into weeks,
Weeks turn into months,
Months turn into years,
Years turn into decades,
Decades turn into an eternity.

Nothing seems to change,
time stands still —
Until one day, it doesn't.

Don't waste your time,
everyday is a new chance to shine.

Get outside and enjoy the views,
video games can wait a minute or two.

Do well in school and pay attention to grades,
you will not soar with F's but you will with A's.

Your parents love you, so don't be mean,
they want to see you smile and succeed.

What is your plan? Do you have a path?
Perhaps something in Science, English, or Math?

It's important to have some fun too.
Play a sport or instrument, maybe the gazoo?

The world is yours to take, new beginnings await.

Tick Tock
Tick Tock
Tick Tock

Manage your time wisely while you can,
A marathon at first, but a sprint at the end.

Make choices that are good for you,
love and live fiercely, that's all you can do.

A Moment in Time

Sweat on your brow.
Heart beating out of your chest.
Tears forming in your eyes.
Worries engulf:
Stop!
Breathe!
Time Out!
Whatever it is, it's only a moment out of your life.
Break it down —
One minute,
One hour,
One day,
Even just one second at a time.
It's normal to be overwhelmed,
but baby steps is the key,
To lock the fear away.
You've got this!

The Elephant in The Room

The elephant in the room takes up the entire space.

The elephant in the room has a weird look on his face.

The elephant in the room stands on the floor.

The elephant in the room can't fit through the door.

The elephant in the room doesn't know how he got here.

The elephant in the room has a presence that's clear.

The elephant in the room is here for a chat.

The elephant in the room can help you with that.

The elephant in the room needs to be addressed.

The elephant in the room is very impressed.

The elephant in the room is proud of you.

The elephant in the room showed you what to do.

The elephant in the room wants to stay.

The elephant in the room will come visit another day.

Puzzles

An orphaned puzzle piece lost in time,
trying to find the place it belongs.

Not ever quite fitting in,
the same, but just a tad different.

Bending to change its shape and design,
to attempt to force its way into the group.

Hopelessly wedging in openings that seem right,
but end up breaking the connection.

Yet, a space is out there somewhere waiting to fill,
and then the missing piece will find joy in acceptance.

The Pilot

Tiny little airplanes circling around my belly.
Preparing to take off into the world.
Soaring
Soaring
Soaring
Embarking on my first big flight.
Head already in the clouds.
Up
Up
Up
Safely and securely exploring.
To pilot towards a new destination.

Confidence

Confidence has the sparkle of precious gemstones.
Positivity is worth your weight in gold.
Bright smiles of happiness shine like diamonds.
Secure like silver chains that shimmer.
Play dress up with a collection of rare jewels.
Not hidden away,
no key needed to unlock.
To value yourself . . .
Is the ultimate treasure.

Rainy Day Naps

Rain on the windows go tap tap tap,
It's a perfect day for a nice long nap.

Snuggle under a blanket by the fire,
All of a sudden I'm very tired.

Some say I'm lazy but that's not fair,
Sometimes a time out is needed self care.

Drift off to sleep and have sweet dreams,
Afternoon naps are what we all need.

Dream Big

Don't shrink behind your immense talents.

You are not too small to reach higher.

Short sighted actions are a tall order to overcome.

Compact mirrors still reflect light.

Tiny voices can have a huge impact.

A little faith goes a long way.

Oh Dear Wee One,

you have permission to DREAM BIG!

True Bestie

All I want is a true bestie,
someone who gets and understands me.

I have friends, don't get me wrong,
but not the one who guides me along.

Play, jump, and run all day,
trust they'll protect what I say.

I know that friend is out there for me,
when I find them, I'll dance with glee.

Until then, I will be nice to all,
and hope my bestie answers the call!

Friendship Bracelets

Friendship bracelets made of string,
At the end of the day, don't mean a thing.
When rude girls get their way,
Create rumors meant to betray.
So keep your trinkets for what they are,
Evidence of a middle school battle scar.
This is normal and true in life.
All you can do is fight internal strife.
Be the absolute best friend that you can be.
All will make some sense eventually.

Rubber Bands & Bonds

Middle School friendships can be like rubber bands.
Tough and resilient one day,
bouncing back from whatever stretches thin from within.
A bond never to be broken.
But other times the tension is too great,
and the union starts to fray.
The harder it's pulled apart,
the more pressure is endured.
Until one day, it just snaps.
And when that happens,
it stings.
But ice your wounds.
True friends are out there waiting for you.

Middle School Monarchy

Fog envelops the castle
Thick haze of insecurity lingers
A mystery to all who enter
Myths & rumors plague
Testimonials of character
Unkindness of heart
Kings and Queens rule with sharp tongues
Commoners judged in a different kind of court
Royal Balls replaced with dances and formals
Peerage of popularity rises
Monarchy preys on the self conscious
Oh the regal halls of Middle School
Hold your head high and adjust your crown
Those who try to hold you down will fall
And look up to watch you reign supreme

Tough Stuff

My worries tend to vary,
and are sometimes scary,
but I know it's temporary.

There are things that help my doubts,
no longer need to scream and pout,
just breathe deep, in and out.

Count slowly - One, Two, Three,
the rhythm grabs and steadies me,
settling down so I can see.

My favorite blankee is here to clutch,
when my tummy's in a rut,
calms me down right to the touch.

I feel the soft fabric start to fray,
from twirling it around all day,
having it with me means I'm ok.

Through the window, see stars up high,
they wink above me, in the sky,
watch over at night so I don't cry.

Being anxious is tough stuff but I am too,
someday this will all be through,
there is nothing that I can't do.

The Talent Path

So many talents, every kid on a tear,
hard not to compare my path to theirs.

Some can gleefully hum and sing,
yet, harmonizing is not really my thing.

There are others who are born to dance,
with my two left feet, there's not a chance!

Others have an eye and passion for art,
I can't say that lives in my heart.

Or such raw emotion in the school play,
my feelings don't tend to come out that way.

If you can dunk a Basketball,
you are instantly the hero of the halls.

The pretty girls who tumble and cheer,
have the popularity we hold so dear.

Maybe I could try a sport with a stick,
sooner or later something has to click.

Not like I can dive or swim,
can't make that team on a whim.

The kids who hit the home runs,
are the ones having the most fun.

I guess I have time to figure out my lane,
once I do, will have so much to gain.

I am just a kid after all,
someday I will confidently stand tall.

It's only a matter of time,
Until I find that one thing that's mine!

The Mental Test

When I melt down, my parents don't spank me,
when I don't listen, there are few time outs.
They pull me aside and ask me to be,
clear with what it's all about.

My parents care to know what I'm going through,
and try their best to help me relax.
Even though they get frustrated too,
it's best to breathe through the panic attack.

Once things are calm and even again,
we write down triggers to prepare.
So we know what to expect and count to ten,
they understand this and are aware.

That it's not my fault and this too shall pass,
my parents surely know what's best.
And the time goes by very fast,
when you are hugged and loved through a mental test.

Mental Movie

When I close my eyes for the day,
that's when the mental movie plays.

A collection of memories in my mind,
that continues to loop & rewind.

Remember my first soccer goal or that A in math,
or the time I was a mermaid in the bath.

When I sing and dance in the car,
when my imagination takes me far.

So many special times, close to keep,
while I try to fall asleep.

In my head, replay recurring themes —
A peaceful way to enter my dreams.

Buddy Bench

Wish my worries would flee,
like winter leaves on the trees.

Would like to make a new friend,
at recess, sit on the buddy bench.

Look around at all the fun,
kids loudly chat as they weave and run.

Don't know what I would even say,
I guess I just would like to play.

A kid I don't know sees my face,
he asks if I want to join the race.

I suppose I can do that,
honestly, I'm pretty fast.

I'm so glad he came up to me,
making new friends can be easy.

When someone cares and is kind,
It surely can ease the mind.

The Bully Crew

When there is a bully crew,
It says more about them than it does about you.

They are likely unhappy in some way,
and will try to ruin your day.

So keep your head held way up high,
ignore them, look away, and don't reply.

Once the reaction from you is gone,
they will retreat and move along.

They are not worth any of your time,
you are busy with mountains to climb!

Have pity for them as they go,
you are worth much more than you know.

Kaleidoscope

A kaleidoscope of emotions.
Tiny mood beads.
Reds, Blues, Yellows and Greens —
Anger, Sadness, Happiness, Jealousy.
Jumbled, colorful, and beautiful.
Sometimes messy, heavy, and blurry.
Expressed through the power of words.
A series of patterns that change accordingly.
Poetry is the instrument that connects.
To look inside the mirror of oneself,
for a clear reflection of wonder.

Life's Map

"Where am I going and what am I doing?" Life's map holds the answers.

The map of life is not a mystery. It's made just for you. It's not stained or discolored. It's full of vibrant possibilities like an unlocked golden chest at the bottom of the ocean floor.

The map is not ripped or wanted by Pirates like in an adventure movie. It's the warm glow emanating from the Lighthouse to help you see a clear future.

Where there is darkness, the map lights the way. Like stars in the sky, reach for the highest and brightest one to guide.

The map does not lead to hidden treasures or instant wealth. Gemstones and diamonds are not free. They come with hard work, sometimes in the form of sweat and tears.

Learn to steer your boat both in rough seas and calm waters. You are the Captain of the ship.

———

There is not a GPS that leads you step by step. There is nothing robotic about finding out who you are. Mistakes will be made and choices will be tested.

The route is rarely a straight line and paths will wind like canyon roads. Cars that zoom around blind curves without care can crash.

One bad turn can throw you off the edge of greatness. Fasten your seatbelt and enjoy the scenic routes ahead. Mountains are meant to be climbed, but safety gear is needed.

There will be closed roadways and detours to navigate around. Storms may cause damage and the wind howls with warnings.

Study your map. If you know the ins and outs and back roads, it can lead you to rainbows after the rain.

———

Life's map can also lead you to amusement. There can still be time for fun and games. Work hard and play harder.

Use your map to plot which rides you want to try. Life is a roller coaster of different feelings and the twists and turns can be exciting.

A carousel of options continues to spin. Claw machines can grab opportunities to help you grow.

Take risks but have fun too. Take a spin on the Ferris Wheel of wonder and soar to new heights.

Feed your soul with imagination and big ideas. Sweet Cotton Candy dreams are within reach.

———

Ultimately, you are planning this trip. Life's map is your compass. Will you go North, South, East or West?

The symbols will lead you in the right direction, on a much greater scale. Who you are and who you want to be can be found.

The key to unlock your destination is on your map. No two maps are the same. You can not compare yours to another.

Remember to stick to the route. Ride off into the sunset with confidence and curiosity to achieve your goals.

"Where am I going and what am I doing?" Life's Map holds the answers.

The Current

Teetering on the edge,
Overlook the calm water,
dip a toe into the unknown.
Before long, completely submerged in the deep end.
Only I don't sink . . .
Rise to the surface and float,
while looking above at the clouds.
As I travel to where the current takes me.

Cloud Travel

Sometimes it's tough to have hope.
Find different ways for me to cope.

Like looking at life from bottom to top,
Find calm and relief and then never stop.

If I could float away on a fluffy cloud,
it would be so fun, I'd laugh out loud.

A magic pillow way up high,
that lets you travel through the sky.

Would ride the one that looks like a horse,
I would gallop around the sun, of course.

Or what about the one that looks like a bunny,
hopping from cloud to cloud would be funny.

But maybe the white puffy looking race car,
will speed through the air near and far.

Clouds come in all sizes and shapes,
use your imagination and adventure awaits.

Daydreaming can help you get around,
to a distant land that calms you down.

One Day

One day, you'll find your people.
One day, they will embrace you.
One day, the big fish will flounder.
One day, you will emerge from the depths.
One day, your talents will shine through.
One day, your star will be the brightest in the galaxy.
One day, you'll know exactly who you are.
One day, the opinions of others won't matter.
One day, your story will be written.
One day, the ink will dry on a fan favorite.
And it will be a classic.

Transformations

An ugly duckling to a swan.
A frog to a prince.
A mermaid to a human.
A pumpkin to a coach.
Real life transformations are not fairy tales.
They are complicated and take hard work.
To change yourself from within to grow and mature,
not cut from the cloth of fantasy but from reality.
To be the best version of yourself you can be,
without the help of a magic wand.

Picasso Problems

My nose has a bump,
How I long for a cute petite bridge.

My eyes are the color of mud,
How I long for a sparkling ocean blue gaze.

My smile is a bit crooked.
How I long for a straight diamond grin.

My cheeks are pretty puffy,
How I long for high chiseled cheekbones.

Even still, I am unique and it could be worse.

I could have been created by Picasso.

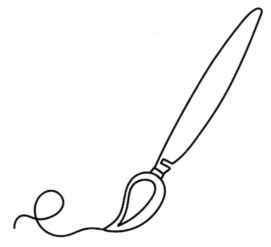

Bicycle of Life

On the bicycle of life,
it's normal to sometimes wobble.
Veer back and forth across lanes of traffic,
gripping the handle bars with fear,
yet, somehow still in control.
Narrowly escaping situations that can hurt.
Protective gear for body and mind is the law,
not a choice.
A destination can sometimes be blocked,
need to look both ways before making a move.
But once the ride gets going,
it can be an exhilarating display of independence.
Follow the rules of the road and
find ultimate balance in unexpected places.

Running

Running towards open arms,
to those who believe in me and what I can accomplish.

Running away from things that scare,
fears that plague my insecurities and affect my confidence.

Running to escape bullies who don't play fair,
being myself makes me the winner in games of nonsense.

Running to free myself from responsibilities,
to just be a kid who laughs with friends.

Running to help someone in need.
when bad things happen, be a helper.

Running to feel the wind in your hair,
the feeling of freedom tickling my nose.

Running to find myself,
through the fields of the forgotten in plain sight.

Running in the light of a bright future,
hopes and dreams take hard work.

With the past in my rear view,
anything is possible.

Work of Art

A work of art,
ahead of your time.
Might not be appreciated by all,
but the moment will come.
Have a unique look and features,
untraditional.
A canvas smeared with questions,
but you have the answers.
Stare over and over again,
you are different.
A display unsure of yourself.
Yet -
Colors fade with purpose.
Creating shades of emotion.
A response to this rare piece who has a place in the world,
even if your value has not been fully understood.
You will find a home someday,
and fit right into the mix.
The days of misunderstanding in the past,
now truly accepted and loved and held up with pride.

Please Talk

When you say everything is fine, but it's not fine.

When you say you are good, but you're not good.

When you say it's no big deal, but it's a big deal.

When you say you can handle it, but you can't handle it.

When you say you don't want to talk, but you DO want to talk.

Please talk!
Please don't hurt alone.
Please ask for help.
Please know you are loved.

Your Story

Your story is still being written—
Blank pages are ok.
Ink runs dry on the day to day.
Differing opinions are acceptable,
A book club of debate.
For the pages to be stuck together is normal.
Not knowing exactly what you want to say is to be expect-
ed.
You are still learning, growing, and finding your place in the
world.
Someday you will be right where you are supposed to be.
A spot on the shelf of greatness!
Your words will influence and comfort.
Life chapters will evolve and captivate.
A classic!
Work hard, dream big, and stay in the right lane.
Write a good one!
Your story will be read with wonder!

Flashlight Haiku

Searching for purpose,
A flashlight into my life,
Shines with potential.

Path Acrostic

Paths are an important part of life.

Allow you to find your way to make dreams come true.

Treat yourself kindly and do not let anyone derail your route.

Have your best interests in mind and secure a bright future.

Path Haiku

Your path will take you,
Wherever you want to go,
Don't veer off the course.

Author Biography

Stephanie lives with her family in Southeastern, Pennsylvania, but is originally from Central, New Jersey where she studied Communications at Rider University. She is back at Rider pursuing a Certificate in Publishing and Professional Writing. Her background is in Advertising/Marketing and most of her writing experience is through those professional roles. Writing and storytelling has been her passion for a long time. She has had several children's poems published by The Dirigible Balloon and Buzgaga online, among others. She also writes the occasional "grown up" piece and has been published online and in print.

Stephanie enjoys reading, theater, mindless web searching, Netflix binges, sunflowers, sports and anything related to coffee!

Acknowledgements

Putting together this poetry book has been one of my life's biggest dreams realized. I have always wanted to be a writer for children. It is my goal to help kids through my words and instill Social Emotional Learning (SEL) concepts that will help them navigate the challenges of adolescence.

I would like to thank my mom in Heaven, who was the first person who ever told me that I should and actually could become a writer. I was eight years old at the time and her words will always be special to me.

Thank you to my family for their patience and support as I wrote this book. My children are my everything and this would not be possible without their influence.

Ingrid Wilson of Experiments in Fiction (EIF) has been a fabulous publishing affiliate and collaborator on this project.

Thank you to Rider University for giving me a second chance to finish what I started. Many thanks to the English Department for keeping me challenged and validated as a writer.

Thank you to the Dirigible Balloon for being the first online publication to publish my Children's poetry, some of which appear in this book.

Thank you to Move Me Poetry for giving me poetic confidence and a home for my words.

Thank you to everyone who has shown kindness and encouragement throughout this process.

Finally, I appreciate everyone who has taken the time to read this collection to their children. It is my hope that they find their place in the world and continue "In the Right Lane" on the road to success and happiness.

Printed in Great Britain
by Amazon

13070072R00071